Cleansing Your Heart
of Anger and Bitterness

Cleansing Your Heart
of Anger and Bitterness

Ernie Gruen

Old Mountain Press

Published by:
Old Mountain Press, Inc.
2542 S. Edgewater Dr.
Fayetteville, NC 28303

www.oldmountainpress.com

Copyright © 2005 Ernie Gruen
Interior text design by Tom Davis
ISBN: 1-931575-54-1
Library of Congress Control Number: 2005920606

Cleansing Your Heart of Anger and Bitterness

First Edition
Printed and bound in the United States of America by Morris Publishing • www.morrispublishing.com • 800-650-7888
1 2 3 4 5 6 7 8 9 10

This book is dedicated to all those who have discovered the secret, that holiness includes having perfect love for every person you have ever known from childhood to the present.

Acknowledgments

Much gratitude goes to all those who helped with valuable editing and making significant suggestions. First and foremost, special thanks is given to my wife, Delores, who tirelessly read and reread the typed manuscript.

I thank the Lord for:
- Lauren Conard who made the book possible by transcribing cassettes on to computer disks;
- Jim and Joy Grainge, long time friends, who joyfully edited the manuscript;
- And, finally, attorney Jim Conard who used his considerable expertise and writing skills to edit, suggest choice of words, and propose clarification when the manuscript was vague.

~~~~~~~~~~~~~~~~~~~

This book is a revision of several tapes preached on the topic of forgiving others during my pastorate (1996-2003) at Faith Fellowship of Love located in Osawatomie, Kansas.

CONTENTS

Cleansing Your Heart of Anger

This could be the most important book you will ever read! I will be exploring how to cleanse your heart of the spirits of anger, disappointment, resentment, hurts, bitterness, hate, revenge, or putting it in different words, cleansing your heart of moaning and mourning. Almost no one will admit to hating someone. We change words to avoid conviction so we do not have to deal with unforgiveness.

One lady announced to me that she did not hate anyone. I asked, "Has anyone hurt you?" She replied, "Hundreds of people have hurt me!" The issue was not simply her choice of words, or semantics; it was that she was deceiving herself. We choose all sorts of words to describe our unforgiveness such as anger, wounds, disillusionment, hurts, bitterness, resentment, and offenses.

The current word to describe out-of-control anger is rage! Regardless of which word we choose, it demonstrates that we have spiritual work to do to have a clean and pure heart full of love.

It is interesting that the church takes a stand against obvious sins like adultery, fornication, uncleanness, lewdness, envy, murders, drunkenness, dissensions, heresies, selfish ambitions and sorcery, but the hidden part of the iceberg is hatred. If God is love, then Satan must be hate! The very essence of the makeup and spirit of Satan is hatred! Look at this very familiar Scripture: "Beloved, let us love one another, for love is of God; and everyone who loves is born of God and knows God. He who does not love does not know God, for God is love— 1 John 4:7-8(NKJV)."

The Parable of the Unforgiving Servant

Let me begin by giving you a Biblical example of how Jesus dealt with unforgiveness. A key passage is the story of the "Parable of the Unforgiving Servant". Study and meditate on its meaning carefully!

Matt 18:21—Then Peter came to Him and said,

"Lord, how often shall my brother sin against me, and I forgive him? Up to seven times?"

22 Jesus said to him, "I do not say to you, up to seven times, but up to seventy times seven.

23 Therefore the kingdom of heaven is like a certain king who wanted to settle accounts with his servants.

24 And when he had begun to settle accounts, one was brought to him who owed him ten thousand talents *(AMP—probably 10 million dollars)*.

25 But as he was not able to pay, his master commanded that he be sold, with his wife and children and all that he had, and that payment be made.

26 The servant therefore fell down before him, saying, Master, have patience with me, and I will pay you all.'

27 Then the master of that servant was moved with compassion, released him, and forgave him the debt.

28 "But that servant went out and found one of his fellow servants who owed him a hundred denarii *(AMP – about twenty dollars)*; and he laid

hands on him and took him by the throat, saying, 'Pay me what you owe!'

29 So his fellow servant fell down at his feet and
begged him, saying, 'Have patience with me,
and I will pay you all.'

30 And he would not, but went and threw him into
prison till he should pay the debt.

31 So when his fellow servants saw what had been
done, they were very grieved, and came and
told their master all that had been done.

32 Then his master, after he had called him, said to
him, 'You wicked servant! I forgave you all that
debt because you begged me.

33 Should you not also have had compassion on
your fellow servant, just as I had pity on you?'

34 And his master was angry, and delivered him to
the torturers (tormentors) until he should pay all
that was due to him.

35 "So My heavenly Father also will do to you if
each of you, from his heart, does not forgive his
brother his trespasses." NKJV

Peter asked Jesus a very important question,
"How often shall by brother sin against me and I

forgive him? Peter thought he was being very magnanimous by suggesting seven times—the number of perfection. But Jesus shocks Peter (and us) by replying, "Not seven times but seventy times seven!" Now consider this: if you forgive the same person 490 times, you have established a <u>habit</u>. Jesus is saying, in effect, that there is no end to the responsibility of forgiving those who have "sinned against us!"

Jesus then tells a story to illustrate his teaching. Let me title it this time, "The parable of the Unforgiving Debtor"! Key points in the parable are:

- The King in settling accounts with his servants finds a man who has such a huge debt (10 million dollars) that he will never be able to pay it. The judgment is that the debtor and his family are to be put in slavery—debtors' prison, if you will.
- The debtor falls on his face and begs for patience and mercy.
- The King is moved with compassion and releases and forgives him the enormous debt.
- The forgiven servant is unwilling to forgive a twenty dollar debt to a fellow servant, and

instead of showing mercy is extremely harsh—grabbing him by the throat and throwing him into prison.

- Some servants tattletale to the King what had transpired; this causes the King to go ballistic and become very angry.
- The unforgiving debtor is delivered to the tormentors or torturers.
- Then the scary (for us!) punch line of the parable is found in verse 35 (KJV): "So likewise shall my heavenly Father do also unto you, if ye from your hearts forgive not every one his brother their trespasses."

I am sure you have figured out the interpretation of the parable, but just in case it went over your head, here is the explanation:

1) The King in the parable is the Lord Jesus Christ, the King of Kings.
2) The Debtor is you and me.
3) The Debt is our sins, along with the resulting guilt and shame.

4) The King, being moved with compassion, refers to Calvary where Jesus died as our substitute, paying the price for our sin and guilt, thereby forgiving and releasing us from our debt.

5) The unforgiving servant represents all who will not forgive others.

6) Unforgiveness allows tormentors or demons permission to torture us. The devil loves and understands this passage; he knows his scriptural and "legal" authority to torment us.

7) "So likewise shall my heavenly Father do also unto you" means that we will be delivered to the tormentors if we do not forgive everyone from our hearts. This is the Lord's answer to Peter's original question: "How often shall I forgive my brother?"

Peter thought that he was being really generous to forgive seven times! He regarded himself as a magnanimous person, full of mercy. Seven times of forgiveness is enough for any jerk! Yet Jesus says, "Peter, not seven times, but seventy times seven," four hundred ninety times. Do you think that Jesus meant to go get a scroll to keep track until the marks total four hundred and eighty nine—then no more forgiveness? Jesus is saying forgiveness is for infinity! You cannot keep count!

In the parable of the unforgiving debtor, the man had a debt he could not pay! This is true of us: our debt of sin and guilt is so great that we can never pay the debt we owe to God! The point is that our debt of sin, foolishness, rebellion, lawlessness, stupidity, failures, and unfaithfulness, when all stacked up, is so great that we can never pay it. The King could say, "throw them into prison." The prison is hell itself!

But Jesus was moved with compassion and says to us, "I release you, I forgive you." What joyous news the Gospel is! On the cross at Calvary, Jesus the King died in our place bearing our sin. "For Christ also suffered once for sins, the just for the unjust, that He might bring us to God—1 Peter 3:18 (NKJV)."

When was Jesus moved with compassion? When he hung on the cross and all our sin-debt was placed on Him. "**Surely He has borne our griefs and carried our sorrows** . . . **He was wounded for our**

transgressions, He was bruised for our iniquities . . . All we like sheep have gone astray; we have turned, every one, to his own way; **And the LORD has laid on Him the iniquity of us all**—Isaiah 53:4-6(NKJV)." On the cross, Jesus forgave and released us from our ten-million-dollar debt!

In light of the Scriptures, we are thus under obligation to forgive all of those who have hurt us, betrayed us, let us down, lied to us or sinned against us in any way. We do not forgive people because they deserve it. (Many people do not deserve to be forgiven—for example, a rapist or a murderer.) We forgive people because Almighty God has forgiven us!

The Tormentors

The first thing we are going to deal with is the shocking statement that those who do not forgive are delivered to the tormentors. Look again at Matt 18:34-35: "And his lord was wroth, and *delivered him to the tormentors*, till he should pay all that was due unto him. So likewise shall my heavenly Father do also unto you, if ye from your hearts forgive not every one his brother their trespasses." Jesus announces *"so likewise will our heavenly Father"* deliver us to the tormentors. The Greek word translated here as tormentor, *basanistou*, is very interesting. It can be translated jailer, torturer, or tormentor. The jailor extracted the truth by the use of the rack. He was an inquisitor, a torturer; the business of torturing was assigned to him.

The question becomes who or what are the tormentors? The tormentors are all kinds of physical and emotional attacks. The tormentors are many — migraine headaches, colitis, stress, nervousness, heart attacks, allergies, insomnia, ulcers, etc. Although we see them as physical or emotional entities, I believe they involve demonic activity also. Read on and come to your own conclusion. Regardless, forgiveness is a major "way out" of both physical and emotional sickness. Forgiveness, according to Jesus, will **release** us from the jailors and the tormentors. Forgiveness is certainly the starting point for healing. However, we can't conclude that those who are sick or who are suffering, are automatically guilty of not forgiving others.

Eye Opening Examples

Lady Healed of a Goiter

A lady who heard my radio broadcast phoned and announced, "I have a goiter. Would you pray for my healing?" I said, "All right, I'll pray for you right over the phone." I said, "You goiter, I take authority and dominion over you in the name of Jesus Christ, God's Son. I command you to loose her and let her go, now, in Jesus' name." When I said that, a demon spoke to me. (The gift of discerning spirits includes the ability to hear or see in the spirit world.) I can still hear what he said. In a sinister, brazen tone the evil spirit declared, "I don't have to let her go; she has hate in her heart." Then I stopped rebuking and started praying in the Spirit. Immediately, the Lord spoke to me, "Mother and sister-in-law." I asked, "Sister, do you have hate in your heart toward any person in your family?" She said, "Yes, my mother and my sister-in-law," and then she named a third relative. I continued, "Let's pray this way: (notice the Trinity) Father, in the name of Jesus, by the Holy Ghost, drop into my mind the names of those that I need to forgive, those toward whom I have resentment, bitterness, or unforgiveness." I instructed her then to pray for each person individually. "Father, as You forgave me when I did not deserve to be forgiven, so likewise I forgive so-and-so whether he/she deserves it or not, in the name of Jesus." As she prayed, I saw a visualization in my mind's eye. I saw a bright polished hollow chrome cylinder. As I looked down inside of it, I saw the interior covered with filth. As she forgave people, name by name, it became cleaner and cleaner. Finally, there were two specks on the side and one speck on the bottom. I understood — "Sister, you've got three more names." She forgave two more people and the two specks came off the side. I said, "You've got one more to forgive and it is on the bottom of your heart." She answered, "Yes, I know who it is. I forgive that one, too, in the name of Jesus." The last speck disappeared and the cylinder was totally clean. I said, "Now I command you, spirits of resentment, bitterness, hate, and unforgiveness —and you goiter—in the name of Jesus Christ loose her and let her go." She said, "I'm going to vomit." She set the telephone down, ran into the bathroom and vomited, and was instantly delivered of the goiter. This incident illustrates the principle—you cannot <u>heal</u> a demon! You must <u>cast</u> <u>out</u> a demon! The goiter was gone; she was healed!

Healing of Allergies

My first comprehension of the role that demons play in healing came at the close of a Full Gospel Business Men's meeting in Emporia, Kansas. A man came forward for prayer with a fungus growth. I prayed a routine prayer for healing but as I walked away, God spoke to me. "This is a demon." I blinked like a toad in a hail storm! I was shocked and amazed; I could barely believe it! I turned around to the man and said, "I believe that is a demon." He said, "I know it is." That surprised me, too. I rebuked the evil spirit and it left him. This incident was followed by no less than a dozen other people being delivered instantaneously of various allergies such as sinus and asthma through deliverance. It was marvelous! That night changed my ministry!

One of my daughters had a chocolate allergy since birth. After eating only one piece of chocolate candy, or drinking half a glass of chocolate milk, the bend of her elbow and wrist area would break out. We would eliminate chocolate from her diet for a few months, and it would clear up except for one small spot. The other three of our children would be drinking chocolate milk, or having a chocolate candy bar, and she'd say, "Can I have some?" "Well you can have a half of one." She would eat half of a candy bar and begin breaking out with a huge spot on the bend of her elbow and the wrist area. This was the pattern. I had prayed for her healing. My wife had prayed for her healing. We had asked the elders to pray for her healing. Nothing ever changed. After the meeting in Emporia I told my home church, "Allergies can be caused by demons and we need to cast them out." When the invitation was given, my daughter came forward. I said, "You chocolate allergy, in the name of Jesus Christ I command you right now to loose her and let her go." She coughed involuntarily! Within three days her wrist and elbow area completely cleared up. Since that time she's had only one reoccurrence, although she has eaten chocolate in all forms to her heart's desire. One morning about a year after being set free, she came into the kitchen and said, "Daddy, there is a little spot there again." I said, "No, you don't, Satan. Loose her in Jesus' name." She coughed again and it cleared up within a day. We don't have to get hung up over whether an illness is caused by a demon or a sickness, since we have authority over both. We simply rebuked it, "Allergy, I command you to come out in the name of Jesus," it then looses the person and they are healed. Someone else can argue over what it was that disappeared.

Get Off God's Property

In Luke 4:38-39, we read, "Simon's wife's mother was sick with a high fever, and they made request of Jesus concerning her. So Jesus stood over her and ***rebuked the fever,*** and it left her. And immediately she arose and served them. Note that Jesus "rebuked" that fever. This is what we are to do with sickness. We are to <u>rebuke</u> it; we are to stand against it. We are to tell it to get off God's property.

When my brother was in the army, stationed at Fort Riley, Kansas, a soldier crawled along the ledge of their window and came into their room during the night while they were sleeping. My brother woke up and saw the intruder going through his pants pockets. He was terrified, but he sat up in bed, shook his fist and yelled in a foghorn type voice, "You get out of here!" The intruder was startled and jumped out the window. This is what we've got to do with the devil. He is a trespasser. You are a temple of the Holy Ghost, if you are saved, and Satan has no right to walk on God's property. Take authority over him and stop tolerating him! Say to Satan, "Get off God's property in the name of Jesus!"

27

Many people have become confused by thinking that if you call a physical condition a demon that you are accusing the person of being demon possessed. Nothing could be farther from the truth. A person is a triune being created in the image of God; he has a body, a mind, and a spirit. People can have a demon attacking their body even though they are walking with God in the light! I believe an evil spirit causes sinusitis. I have seen precious Spirit-filled Christians who had a sinus problem. They were not backslidden. They were not "demon-possessed" in any sense of the term. But an evil spirit was attacking their bodies. When it was commanded to go in Jesus' name it left. It had no choice but to leave!

Migraine Headaches

Headaches can also be caused by demons. An interesting case clearly involving both the principle of authority over demons and the principle of forgiveness occurred while I was preaching in northern Minnesota at a camp retreat near Canada. I saw a woman in a white dress. The Lord told me, "She has migraine headaches; pray for her healing."

I said, "Sister, you have migraine headaches." In amazement, she confirmed, "That's right."

I commanded, "Migraine headache, in the name of Jesus, loose her and go into the deep." She shook her head and said, "Praise the Lord it's gone!" She had been agonizing for weeks with a constant headache. The next morning at breakfast she told me it was back again. I said, "Well, then it's leaving again. Headache, I take authority over you. In the name of Jesus loose her now." She shook her head and said it was gone. A half hour later she came to me and said the headache was back. I said, "Sister, we have been rebuking the symptom, let's go for the cause."

I asked her to come to our cabin after lunch. Interestingly, she was a preacher's widow. I showed her Matthew 18, and she asked God to reveal to her the names of those she needed to forgive. It took two and a half hours! She named two or three hundred names—many of them church members who had hurt her and her husband, disappointed them, let them down, or criticized them. The hurts and wounds had accumulated until they resulted in her taking medications for migraine headaches and nervousness. But during this process of forgiving everyone, she was instantly healed. We didn't even have to pray for her! Once her heart was cleansed by forgiveness, her healing was permanently secured.

Cancer

All over the country I encounter people to whom God has spoken this same thing—people who have had no contact with me. But they do have a relationship with Jesus, and Jesus has taught them the same thing He taught me. One such person—a lady with cancer—had been prayed for many times and was not healed. She and her husband had a retreat cabin. She had him take her up to their cabin and leave her there. "I'm going to fast and pray for three days," she said. "Then you come and get me." God spoke to her and said, "Get all the hate out of your heart from your childhood up." In those three days she searched her heart and forgave every single person, then was totally healed of cancer. It is hate that keeps the Spirit from flowing; hate can keep a person from being healed.

Curse of Black Magic

A woman phoned who had heard my radio broadcast. "Brother Ernie, they put a curse of black magic on me," she said. I replied, "Well, that is no problem for the blood of Jesus Do you agree with me?" Then I said, "You curse of black magic, I break your power in the name of Jesus by the blood of the Lamb." She called back a few days later and said, "It didn't work." I said, "There is something wrong. I'm going to pray again." She called back a few days later and said, "Brother Gruen, it didn't work." I said, "Sister, the Bible says resist the devil and he will flee from you. There must be something wrong with your resistance." I started praying in tongues to get discernment and then I said, "Do you really want to know what your problem is? It isn't black magic." She disagreed, "Oh yes, it is black magic." I said, "No, it isn't. Do you want me to tell you the truth? It will make you mad." God had given me a word of knowledge. She said, "No, I wouldn't get mad at a servant of the Lord." (And she didn't.) I said, "You've got bitterness in your heart towards whole families of people. Isn't it true?"

It shocked her. She confessed, "It is true." She asked if I was still going to pray for her. I said, "I would be wasting my time unless you do something first." I told her how to pray and go through forgiveness. Then, I said, "When you get through receiving the names, and forgiving, then I will pray for you." She called back about a week later and said, "Brother Gruen, it took me five days to get finished naming the names. I know I had more than five hundred names of people—both living and dead." Her problem was not black magic, but unforgiveness in her heart. Her self-diagnosis was incorrect!

A Woman from Germany with Nervous Breakdowns

Satan has many ways of trying to camouflage hate. We must be alert to prevent being deceived by such a simple trick as switching labels. A woman from Germany called for counseling. She had been to many spirit-filled pastors in the Kansas City area. She had heard about our ministry and thought perhaps I'd have a little more "faith and power" than anyone else. This is a common ailment among full-gospel people; they keep running from preacher to preacher, hoping to find one who will be able to pray the prayer of faith. She announced boldly that God had told her to call me. I was intimidated by the situation, but I thought if God really spoke to her to call me, I would talk to her about forgiveness, because that was the one thing I had a revelation about.

When she arrived, she began by stating, "I have had four nervous breakdowns." I directed her to Matthew 18 and explained the parable of the unforgiving servant. She said with a brogue, in very broken English, "I don't have unforgiveness." She said her problem was a hard life—she had been through World Wars I and II. She even attributed her condition to heredity. I told her, "Sister, I've prayed with hundreds of people all over the United States during the past five years and it is unforgiveness."

She insisted, "I don't have unforgiveness toward anybody." There was no use arguing. So I said, "Sister, I'll tell you what. You love the Lord, don't you?" She affirmed she did. I suggested, "If you did happen to have unforgiveness would you be willing to forgive?" "Why, of course," she replied. "Let's just leave it up to the Holy Spirit," I recommended. She agreed. I had her pray after me, "Father, in the name of Jesus, if there are any people that I have resentment or bitterness or hurt feelings or hate toward, drop their names into my mind, and I will forgive them right now."

I asked her if she received any names. She said, "Na, na, just faces of people." I said, "What do you mean?" She replied, "I see in my mind the village in Germany where I lived and the market place is crowded with all of my acquaintances, and I hate every one of them." It took over two hours for this woman who "didn't have any unforgiveness" to name the names and forgive each one individually. She was a wonderful Christian and was not attempting to deceive. However, she honestly was unaware of the unforgiveness. But the Holy Spirit—the spirit of truth—has a wonderful memory. We can always pray, "Search me, O God, and know my heart: try me, and know my thoughts: and see if there be any wicked way in me, and lead me in the way everlasting—Ps 139:23-24(KJV)."

Hurt Feelings

As I was counseling with another woman she announced, "I don't have resentment toward anyone." The Holy Spirit whispered to me, "She calls it hurt feelings." I asked, "What about hurt feelings?" She said, "Hundreds of people have hurt me." The devil switched labels on her to get her out from under conviction. She forgave her father, mother, husband, children, etc. When she was through forgiving, the power of God went through her. Many testify like this, "I feel like I just got saved again," or "I never have had such peace," or some begin praying in tongues for the first time. God's Spirit is love and love cannot flow when we are filled with hate. Hate is a dam. God wants to pour out His Spirit on us and heal us and make us whole; but He can't if we have the Spirit of God dammed up with bitterness, resentment, wounds, hurts, or hard feelings, that we have stored up through the years. I would estimate that the person going through forgiveness initially will receive from 40 to 400 names or faces.

We've seen hundreds of people stop taking tranquilizers after they cleaned their heart of unforgiveness. If someone tells me they are nervous, I'll turn to Matthew 18 and go through the principle of forgiveness with them. It may take an hour or two, but when we are finished we usually do not have to pray for healing; they are already released!

Sexual Abuse

Many cases are sad and tragic. For example, a Missouri woman in her late forties was taking thirty-two pills a day and going to several doctors called for help. I prayed for her. The Lord revealed to me, "Eight years old." I asked her what had happened to her when she was eight years old. She told me her older brother had molested her. I asked her if she was willing to forgive him. She said he was dead. I said, "That doesn't matter; the resentment isn't."

She named his name, saying, "I forgive you in the name of Jesus. As God forgave me when I didn't deserve it, I forgive you whether you deserve it or not." She then began to cry; and I physically felt the peace of God descend upon her. I said, "Sister, do you feel that?" She said, "Yes." She was released from tranquilizers. An eight-year-old girl can hardly be seductive; she was the innocent party. But here was an innocent woman who had suffered nearly forty years because the devil had planted a root of bitterness in her heart because she hadn't forgiven.

I was praying with a man one day and the Lord revealed to me, "seven years ago." I asked him what happened seven years ago. He said, "Nothing." I said, "The Holy Spirit is not a liar. What happened seven years ago?" Again, he insisted that nothing had happened seven years ago. I said, "You tell me the truth in Jesus' name." He shrieked, "I hate him!" as loudly as he could scream. Another man had committed adultery with his wife seven years before. I told him he had to forgive the man. He said, "He doesn't <u>deserve</u> to be forgiven." I looked him right in the eye and said, "Neither did <u>you</u>." We have been forgiven a ten-million-dollar debt. God has loved us and put up with us and forgiven us over and over. So how can we do anything but forgive and love every other person?

Financial Wounds

When God showed me the truth about unforgiveness, I just knew I didn't have any unforgiveness. I am not a person to hold grudges and I felt sure that I didn't hold any resentment. But I prayed, "Father, just in case I do have unforgiveness, drop the names into my mind that You see I need to forgive." Eight names hit my mind so quickly that my head swam. What a shock! One name that came to me was that of a man who I believed had cheated my mother out of her life savings by claiming bankruptcy.

Seemingly Insignificant Things

When you pray, "Father, in the name of Jesus, by the Holy Spirit, drop into my mind the names or faces of those persons from childhood up to this present time that I need to forgive," you are in for some surprises. One woman said that her uncle came to her mind. I feared the worst scenario. But when I asked what her uncle had done to her, she replied that he tickled her every time that he saw her. She couldn't stand to be tickled; it was pure torture. The problem can be as insignificant as tickling or having your hair pulled in elementary school. But whatever it is, you must forgive that person.

Racial Wounds

Some of you have been wounded deep down in your spirit. If you have deep wounds, you may need someone to pray with you further, lay hands on you and ask the Holy Spirit to heal your broken heart. Jesus said, "I have come to heal the broken-hearted. I have come to set at liberty those that are bruised" (Luke 4:18). I was teaching at an African-American camp in Kansas City, Kansas. A precious elderly black saint in her eighties came forward for prayer. As I began to pray, I saw her spirit, and it looked as if it had been chopped into a hundred pieces by an onion chopper. I said, "Lord, what does it mean?" He said, "She has been chopped and hurt and wounded just like that in her spirit, and your race did it." I stood there and wept. God said, "You ask her for forgiveness as a representative of the white race."

I said to my sister, "This is what I see your spirit is like..." Then I asked, "As a representative of the white race, will you forgive us?" She began to cry also. She said, "I forgive you." The Holy Spirit went through her like a bolt of electricity from the top of her head to the toes of her feet, and she was made whole!

We don't understand the wounds and heartaches that some people have. Some of them have been through multiple marriages. They need someone to love them, to cry with them and to pray with them. The baptism in the Holy Spirit should give us sensitivity, patience, and understanding so we can minister forgiveness to the needs of people.

The Nature of Our Problem

One day while I was visiting with an acquaintance she mentioned to me during the course of our conversation that she was taking tranquilizers. I said, "Sister, you have heard me preach on this. You know what is behind those nerves." "Yes," she said, "and I know whom I hate. It's my father-in-law, and I'm going to keep on hating him." I said, "Well, you will have to keep on taking your pills then." She was in an unrepentant attitude that day, but a few days later she prayed and forgave him. Then the nervousness left; the tranquilizers left, too.

Are you beginning to comprehend why people aren't healed? They are delivered to the tormentors because of unforgiveness. You see, when the devil said to me that day, "I don't have to let her go," he knew his rights scripturally. The devil knows whether he has a legal basis to attack or torment a person. When my wife, Delores, and I begin to pray for someone's deliverance, we'll start by rebuking the particular tormentor. If it doesn't bring results, we turn to Matthew 18. We know it is impossible to get a person really free who has hate in any form in their heart. **Hate is a doorkeeper—the strong man.** After the person understands the message of forgiveness and specifically prays through forgiveness, then we command the spirits of resentment, bitterness, and unforgiveness to leave. Other problems must leave also.

If you forgive everybody of everything from your earliest childhood memories to the present, you will have nothing left but love in your heart. You will never have greater love than this: forgiving someone who doesn't deserve to be forgiven, for that is what Jesus did for us on the cross. Love is forgiveness! We show the love of Jesus Christ when we pray what He prayed on the cross, "Father, forgive them; for they know not what they do." God is love. Satan is hate. We've majored on minors such as smoking, dancing, and drinking—and I don't believe in any one of the three—but when have you heard a sermon on resentment? We major on minors, and minor on majors! The very nature of the devil is hate; the very essence of sin is hate. The very core of our sin problem is anger, hate, bitterness, resentment, envy, malice, hurt feelings, etc. If you want to be healed in your spirit and mind and body—you must be sincere and ask the Father in the name of Jesus to give you the names or faces of those whom you need to forgive. The Holy Spirit has a good memory. It may take you two or three hours or longer to pray for each person one by one. In addition, it is not uncommon to receive some names during the following days.

Pray specifically for each person God gives you and choose to forgive just as you have been forgiven—whether they deserve it or not. Don't do a quickie job of praying! Pray for each person's salvation and well-being. Ask God to give you His love for the person, because your love is inadequate. Search your heart to see what part you had in the offense. Many times we are partly to blame.

Thirty days after I preached on forgiveness in one full-gospel church people were saying, "God is still dealing with me about forgiveness." It was a Bible-believing church, yet full of bitterness. That is sad. We are kidding ourselves if we say we are full of the Holy Spirit and at the same time we are hating our spouse or our child or our mom or our neighbor or our boss. It does not matter whether someone cheated you out of money, was unfaithful to you, or let you down when you depended on them; you must forgive them. If you don't forgive, you will pay a terrible price. It will cost your mental health, your physical health, and your spiritual well-being. Since you have more light, now you have some more praying to do! The core of reality is love. If we have anything against anyone in our family, our neighborhood, our church, our childhood, or if we feel something between that person's spirit and our spirit, then we need to pray and get the resentment and bitterness out of us. We need to pray until we have perfect love for every person in the world. When love flows, the Spirit of God flows, and when the Spirit flows, healing and deliverance are manifested.

Prayers Blocked

"For assuredly, I say to you, whoever says to this mountain, 'Be removed and be cast into the sea,' and does not doubt in his heart, but believes that those things he says will be done, he will have whatever he says. Therefore I say to you, whatever things you ask when you pray, believe that you receive them, and you will have them—Mk 11:23-26 (NKJ)." Jesus, in this famous passage, taught about the power of prayer. But Jesus was NOT through speaking. He continues, "**And whenever you stand praying, if you have anything against anyone, forgive him**, that your Father in heaven may also forgive you your trespasses. But if you do not forgive, neither will your Father in heaven forgive your trespasses." Do you know why we don't have faith? H-A-T-E: resentment and bitterness. How dare we stop in the middle of a passage; faith and forgiveness work together!

When you pray, the first names you will receive are those who are very close to you—the people you love most. You will get the name of your spouse, mother, father, and the names of your children. You may have resentment toward one child. This is typically because the child is so much like you, and you see yourself in them.

When the Holy Spirit gives you a name, it does not mean that you don't also love that person. It simply means that because of your close relationship Satan has tried to cause a division between the two of you. When your family member irritates you, then forgive them immediately. It isn't that you don't love them; it's just that where there is a little resentment, a little bitterness can grow and develop. Maybe your wife is a nagger or perhaps your husband is inconsiderate or maybe your father wasn't affectionate. For example, while talking with a sister I asked, "What kind of relationship did you have with your father?" She said she didn't know him. "You mean he left home?" "No," she replied, "he was there. He provided for us, but I didn't really know him. He never held me, never showed any affection and never expressed real care for me." Don't let little resentments grow in family relationships. Forgive fully, allow the bitterness to be removed by the Holy Spirit, and then move on.

Estrangement

A man who had heard our radio broadcast called and explained that although they shared a house, he and his wife had been estranged for nearly a year. You don't need much discernment to know a marriage like that is in deep trouble. I visited them, opened the Bible to Matthew 18 and went through it with them. I then said to the husband, "You're the head of the home. Do you want to start?" He said, "Father, in the name of Jesus drop into my mind the names of those I need to forgive." He began to cry and got choked up. Kneeling there he sobbed, "Daddy, I forgive you in the name of Jesus." Then he turned to his wife, put his arms around her and said, "Honey, I forgive you in the name of Jesus." Tears of healing flooded down his cheeks as the dam of resentment burst. An hour later they were through their initial list of names. A year later, the wife wrote me a letter thanking me. She wrote, "We've had a brand new marriage ever since that Saturday morning when we forgave each other." Praise God!

The Root Problem

Whatever our physical or emotional problem is, we must go to the <u>root</u> spiritual cause. Tormentors that come can be the consequences of unforgiveness. Preachers teach on the surface; then we pray on the surface; consequently our salvation isn't very deep. Surface dealing with tormentors is like a lawnmower mowing down wild Johnson grass. We mow it off only to have it grow back again. The wild grass must be killed at the roots. So, likewise, we must get at the root of a person's problems. We should ask for the cleansing with the blood of Jesus very specifically, instead of the usual vague generic prayers.

For example, a lady came for prayer for her marriage. She was not having a satisfactory relationship with her husband. The Lord spoke to me, "Age thirteen." Her father had molested her. With tears streaming she chose to forgive her father. She asked the blood to cleanse her of hatred towards him, towards men in general and towards the sexual relation in marriage. She not only received a new marriage relationship, but also reported that she no longer resented her little boy. She had resented him simply because he was a male. We had prayed with her on the root level rather than a quickie surface prayer. Consequently, her solution was deep and complete—not superficial and shallow.

Psychology can expose roots but without the blood of Jesus there is no way to experience cleansing or healing. When the sinful attitude is discovered and then removed by Jesus' blood, wholeness and transformation can take place. Now we can understand the absurdity of Peter's question, "Lord, how oft shall I forgive my brother, until seven times?" **Forgiveness is not optional; it is an absolute imperative and is to be as limitless as God's love.**

Hate Destroys

Even if I were a non-Christian, I still would not let hatred fill my heart because of what I know. I do not want to be destroyed. Hatred <u>destroys</u> you. Bitterness <u>destroys</u> you. Resentment <u>destroys</u> you. It is extremely self-destructive to hate. If you resent someone, they may not even know it. That person may be as happy as a lark, but you'll be eaten up, destroying yourself with headaches, nerves and insomnia. Isn't that stupid? Nobody is more foolish than someone who lets hate ruin his life. **Hated is cancer of the soul!**

Did you ever notice the serious wording in the Lord's Prayer? "Lord, forgive my debts as I forgive..." Are you sure you want to pray the Lord's Prayer? After Jesus finished the prayer, He decided to add one important statement of clarification, "For if you forgive men their trespasses, your heavenly Father will also forgive you. **But if you do not forgive men their trespasses, neither will your Father forgive your trespasses.** (Matthew 6:14-15)." What we are praying in reality is, "Lord, if I do not forgive, please send me to hell!"

Forgiveness is not an Option

God has placed this book in your hands by divine destiny. Don't let the devil rob you of the need to forgive from your heart. Reading this book will be a waste of time if you do not diligently go through forgiveness. But if you've prayed what the Scriptures have said, you'll be a brand new person on the inside. You'll never be the same! Up to this point we have discussed the absolute imperative of forgiveness. Having been forgiven of so much by our wonderful Lord Jesus Christ, we see that we can do nothing else but forgive all those who have wounded us. Forgiveness is not optional; it is an absolute must. It is time to let hurts, wounds, and revenge go. Let it go! Lay it down once for all!

How to Forgive

We must understand that forgiveness is not an emotion. It is a _decision_ you make in prayer. You may or may not feel something. Forgiveness is a _choice_ you make before God in prayer. Forgiveness is not mental or emotional gymnastics in your soulish realm. Jesus said in John 14:14, "If ye shall ask anything in my name, I will do it." Read this verse as if the Jesus Himself were speaking directly to you, "If you ask anything in my name, I will do it." Now let us suppose that you have a deep resentment for a relative. You do not have to pretend that you really do not have resentment, but quite the opposite. Go right to God, admit it and confess it for what it is. You should pray in this manner:

"Dear Lord Jesus, You know that I hate _____, but this resentment (hatred, anger, bitterness, etc.) is sin. I ask you to wash away this sin with your blood. As a definite act of my will, I choose to forgive them whether they deserve it or not. You forgave me when I didn't deserve it, and so likewise I forgive them. Jesus, I ask You to give me your love for them, because mine is inadequate. You promised me in Your Word if I asked anything in Your name, You would do it. I have asked You to cleanse this resentment out of me and You have. I have asked You to give me Your love for them, and so now I have Your love for them."

Your faith is **based on two things**: 1) in the power of the blood of Jesus to cleanse you, and 2) in the Scripture in John 14:14, "If ye shall ask anything in my name, I will do it." Your faith is **not based** on your emotions or your feelings, but Scripture.

Continue to pray deeply in reference to each person who has offended you. You might ask God to give you a tender and kind spirit instead of a harsh, critical attitude. You may ask the Lord to save them if they have not yet been born-again. You might pray earnestly for their deliverance from evil spirits if you sense that to be a need. Remember, the Scriptures teach that, "We wrestle not against flesh and blood, but against principalities, powers, rulers, and evil spirits — (Ephesians 6:12)." Do not cut your prayer short, continue to pray as the Holy Spirit leads you, focusing on this one situation. Do a thorough job, praying until the Holy Spirit bears witness that you are finished. Now, follow the same procedure for each name or face that the Holy Spirit drops into your mind. Yes, it may take hours and maybe days to completely clear your heart and spirit of resentment, anger, bitterness, and offenses. Remember that your salvation will never go any deeper than your repentance.

After having prayed thoroughly in the above manner, you will be free of bitterness toward each person and will have the love of Jesus for them. If you are not convinced of this, the problem is no longer unforgiveness but unbelief.

I remember an experience requiring forgiveness in my own life. I was deeply hurt by a group of my closest Spirit-filled brothers in a church where I was pastoring. I was at the point of quitting the ministry. I said in my heart, "They can take that church and run with it. Phooey on the whole bunch of them. I don't have to put up with this. I am quitting the ministry. I don't care anymore. And I don't care that I don't care; I don't even want to care." But I knelt down to pray and I said, "Lord, I know that this mood I am in is not of Your Holy Spirit, and I **choose** for You to change me, even though I do not want to change."

My wife was also deeply hurt. She is a registered nurse and she prayed, "Lord, I believe your blood is so powerful that it can even heal us in our inner man. There are two kinds of wounds, one with suture marks and one without a scar. So with Your blood, heal us in our spirits so that there will not even be a scar left." God did it. He healed us in our inner man. We chose against both our will, and our emotions!

The day of sorrow has been one of the most glorious days of my life, because through it God worked sensitivity into my heart. "Sorrow is better than laughter, for by a sad countenance the heart is made better—(Eccl 7:3)." "Blessed are those who mourn, for they shall be comforted —(Matt 5:4)."

Let me reiterate that forgiveness is something we choose to do in prayer; it is not an emotion. In fact, one of the most important principles for a Christian to grasp is that <u>*we can choose against our own will*</u>. A secret of prayer is that when we choose something in Jesus' name, then the Holy Spirit is released by God inside our inner man to change us in accordance with our request. It is marvelous news to find out that even our <u>will</u> can be changed; our human will is replaced by God's divine will!

It sounds like a paradox to say that one can choose against his own will; but in reality this is the power of prayer. We are not left dependent upon our own ability or strength. The real issue is not feelings, but whether we choose to forgive. If we choose to be willing, God has promised to change our desires. "For it is God who is at work in you, both to will and to work for His good pleasure (NAS)." Or as the New Living Translation renders it, "For God is working in you, giving you the desire to obey him and the power to do what pleases him (Phil. 2:13)." This is not only the secret of forgiveness; it is also the secret of being delivered from any attitudes or habits that are contrary to the will of God. You can be delivered from smoking, evil desires, selfishness, gluttony, jealousy, domination, drunkenness, a rebellious attitude, an adulterous spirit, gossip, backbiting, anger, lying, or any other sin, because when you call on God in Jesus' name to change you, then the Holy Spirit is released to do His work in you.

Also, we must forgive ourselves. It is a sin to not love yourself. The second of the two great commandments states, "Love your neighbor as yourself." There is a proper self-love. It is a self-love that involves self-respect, not selfishness. The Scripture teaches in Hebrews 10:17, "Your sins and iniquities will I remember no more." If you knelt down to re-confess some particular, grievous sin. God would say to you, "What are you talking about?" You might reply, "God, don't you remember?" And God would say, "Frankly, no. I have forgotten it, now you forget it also, my child." If the Judge of heaven and earth declares you forgiven, it is the height of presumption and pride for you, on your part, to not forgive yourself. It would be elevating yourself above God. Therefore you should simply pray a prayer like this:

"Dear Jesus, You have forgiven me and have forgotten my sin. I am not higher than You. Therefore, I choose likewise to forgive myself and to forget my sin. With Your blood wash away all my guilt and shame and even the remembrance of the guilt of my sin, in Jesus' name. Amen.

Finally one other aspect of forgiveness which we need to consider is our attitude towards God Himself. Many people, through sorrows and pains, trials and tribulations, become bitter toward God. Now, it is obvious that God is holy and cannot sin. Consequently, He has not sinned against us, nor failed us. Therefore the problem is not our forgiving God, but rather repenting of our attitude toward God.

We must know that it is literally true that "all things work together for good to them that love God, and to them who are the called according to His purpose" (Romans 8:28). This verse does not teach that everything is good. There are many circumstances and trials that are evil and not good. But this verse states that God causes all things to work together *for good*. It is not what happens to us in life that is important, but our response to what happens to us in life. The same experience can make one person bitter and disillusioned while making another person sensitive and full of compassion for others. Bitterness is a wrong response toward God. Notice also that He causes all things to work together for His purpose. His purpose, according to the next verse, is that we should be "conformed to the image of His Son." The purpose of God is always fuller and richer than our temporal and carnal purposes. He causes everything to work together for ***His purpose*** , not ours.

Therefore we can pray like this:

"God, I know that You are holy and cannot sin. "You do all things well" (Mark 7:37). My attitude toward You has been one of questioning and bitterness. This is sin. I repent of it! Wash me thoroughly from my iniquity, and cleanse me from my sin. Wash this wrong attitude away with Your blood. I realize that all evil comes from Satan, not from You. Forgive me for blaming You for the works of the enemy. I can, and I do trust You. I know that all things do work together for my good. And Father, I love You. In Jesus' name, Amen."

The purpose of this book was to help you in clearing your heart of the spirit of anger, hurts, disappointments, resentments, bitterness, hate, and revenge. Were we successful?

If not, please reread this book, and work your way through forgiveness. On the other hand, if you have sincerely experienced the joy of forgiving others, then pass this book along to a friend so that you can minister to someone else. God bless you!

About the Author

Pastor Ernest J. Gruen is the son of a devout Baptist deacon. He was converted at the age of nine at the Abilene Baptist Church (KS) and called to preach at age 19. He pastored Baptist churches for ten years in the Wichita and Kansas City area. On Christmas night of 1965, Pastor Gruen knew there had to be "something more to Christianity" than what he'd experienced. After praying for five hours, he had a definite second experience of crucifixion and resurrection power—he received the Baptism in the Holy Spirit. This occurred while he was age 29.

ERNIE GRUEN

Pastor Gruen graduated from Friends University in Wichita, Kansas, with honors and received his Masters of Divinity from Central Baptist Seminary in Kansas City, Kansas. He married Delores, his wife, on April 28th, 1956. They have four children and six grandchildren all living in the greater Kansas City area.

He founded Full Faith Church of Love in 1966, which grew to an average Sunday morning attendance of 2,500. This spirit-filled inter-denominational church became a teaching center for the heart of the United States. He managed a staff of over ninety, including twelve pastors, Christian schoolteachers, and support personnel. He pastored that church for twenty-seven years. Pastor Gruen and his churches have always been strongly committed to missions.

He also mentored and discipled younger pastors, while overseeing a network of fifteen churches in the Kansas City area. He provided and oversaw a monthly ministers meeting and annual retreats for these churches. He, with a team, arbitrated conflicts in these churches.

He has been in the ministry for 49 years. He has twenty-eight years of radio experience, with his own daily radio program. He had a weekly television broadcast for eleven years.

He pastored Faith Fellowship of Love in Osawatomie, Ks from 1997 until Dec. 2003. A new season began for his ministry in 2004. The new ministry is "Grace and Mercy Ministries". It is a mobile ministry as God opens doors for him to serve. As a father in the ministry, he has a lot to impart to the Body of Christ. He moves regularly in the gifts of the Word of Wisdom, Word of Knowledge and Prophecy. He bases his ministry out of his home church - Cornerstone Community Church, KC, KS (Pastor Jeff Colleen).

He has ministered extensively in the United States and internationally in Holland, Germany, England, Israel, Kenya, Mexico, Canada, and the former Soviet Union.

Notes

Order Form –May be down loaded from web site
Web page is www.erniegruen.com
E-mail is ejgruen1@juno.com

The author has written six books (all paper backs) and one tract:

Cleansing Your Heart of Anger and Bitterness – Explains how we can deal with those feelings that make us less than we are. [70 pp].

Freedom to Choose – A national best seller; deliverance; principles for victorious living [252 pp].

Freedom to Grow – Appointment with God; confession; encouragement; passing tests [122 pp].

Touching the Heart of God – A detailed analysis of prayer and how to pray practically [288 pp].

The Giver and His Gifts – An analysis of the difference between the New Birth and the Baptism in the Holy Spirit; a detailed discussion of the 25 gifts of the Holy Spirit in the New Test. [308 pp]. Also available in Spanish

A tract entitled: *Have Your Received the Holy Spirit?* Literally thousands have received the Baptism in the Holy Spirit after reading this tract! [11 x 17" sheet, with 8 folds].

But God Gives More Grace – A detailed analysis of the law of humility [112 pp]

- ABSOLUTELY no COD orders, please no exceptions.
- All prices include handling and postage in the continental United States, but please add additional postage for Canada, Mexico, and overseas mailings.

Order Form

Cost Per Book   #of books   Sub-Total

Cleansing Your Heart of
Anger and Bitterness   *$5.00   X_____ = _____

But God Gives More Grace   *$10.00   X _____ = _____

Freedom to Choose   * $7.00   X _____ = _____

Freedom to Grow   * $5.00   X _____ = _____

Touching the Heart of God   * $7.00   X _____ = _____

The Giver and His Gifts   *$15.00   X _____ = _____
* We pay the postage
TRACT:
Have you Received the Holy Spirit?
$3.00 [10 tracts, postage paid] or
$25.00 [100 tracts, postage paid]   X _____ = _____

                                    TOTAL = _____
If order totals $100.00 or more
please subtract 10% discount   = _____

If order totals $200.00 or more
please subtract 25% discount   = _____

                               FINAL TOTAL= _____
Make check payable to : **Grace and Mercy Ministries** and mail to:
Grace and Mercy Ministries, 7819 Twilight Lane, Lenexa, KS 66217-9405
Ship my order to (fill this out please):

Name:_____ Telephone:_____

Address:_____ Telephone:_____

City:_____ State:_____ Zip:_____
E-mail:_____